40 DAYS OF ADORATION PRAYER

BEN WOODWARD

The Better Than

The Savior God

Th Depe...

God Our Mak...

...ace

...ned God

A 40 day journey into the heart of God
through Adoration Prayer.

Taking 40 days to intentionally pray is a bold move. We all have many things screaming for our attention each day and usually the first thing to be discarded is prayer.

But, for those who will take the time to engage with it, there is an invitation to discover God in the place of prayer.

When You said, "Seek My face," my heart said to You, "Your face, O LORD, I shall seek." Psalm 27:8

Staring into someone's face is a very personal thing. It can be awkward and disconcerting if you are the person being looked at. We don't like people staring at us because the longer you stare, the more you see and often what you see is not good.

Staring in to the face of Jesus is different for a number of reasons. Firstly, He never feels awkward and He actually invites your stare. Secondly, the only things you are going to find there are good things.

When so much of our prayer and conversation with Jesus is based around our needs and desires, it can be difficult to just stop and stare. What does that kind of prayer even look like? Are we supposed to just sit in a room and wait?

Staring into the face of God is an invitation into a deeper level of relationship. Just like any earthly relationship, the more you get to know a person's character, the more you can understand them and relate to them. The invitation to stare into the face of God is an invitation into discovering who He is. So the question is, what has He already told us about Himself?

Our primary source of information about who He is comes from the scriptures. What better place is there to start than to take what God has already said about Himself and use that as the foundation for our prayer and communication?

This next 40 days is a journey of prayer based on what God has already told us about Himself in His word. It is using the attributes and character of God as a foundation for our conversation with Him. Instead of asking God for provision, we stare into His face and talk to Him about who He is as a provider. Instead of asking for wisdom, we stare into His nature as the God of wisdom and allow His character to be the foundation of our prayers.

The one thing that I encourage you to remember in the next 40 days is this – Don't ask for a thing! That's not to say that asking in prayer is not valid, but this journey is about discovering who God is, not just trying to get something from Him. I promise you that as you do this, you will find that all your concerns and worries will slowly fade. If you are in need of provision, who better to discover than God the Provider? If you are in need of healing, who better to stare into than God the healer?

Just remember, when you get the King, you also get His Kingdom.

But seek first his kingdom and his righteousness, and all these things will be given to you as well. Matthew 6:33

You are making a bold move! May the next 40 days be a time of hope and encounter as you seek His face.

For more materials on prayer, go to www.benwoodward.com

Ben Woodward

The Better Than

Th The Savior God

Th eepe God Our Make God

God The if ace ned God

HOW DO YOU DO THIS?

1. First and foremost, you need to open your mouth and pray out loud! There is a dynamic interaction that takes place when you actually speak.
2. Don't ask for anything! This "40 days of Adoration Prayer" is designed to focus on who God is not what we need.
3. You can do it in the morning, middle of the day or at night, it doesn't matter when you do it just make the time to do it!
4. When you start, use the written prayers to get you used to the model. As time goes on, begin to add your own words and prayers.
5. Add your thoughts by writing down what you hear from the Lord.

The Savior God

I, even I, am the LORD, and there is no savior besides Me.
Is. 43.11

The Savior God

I, even I, am the LORD, and there is no savior besides Me.
Is. 43.11

Adoration Statement

Jesus, You are my savior! You came and You rescued me from sin and death! Even when I hated you and despised You, You came for me. Even though I deserved punishment for my sin, You took that punishment for me! There is no savior beside You! Just thinking about what You have done for me makes me fall in love You. You are my savior!

Prayer

Lord, as I start this 40 days of adoration prayer, I want to acknowledge what You have done for me. You are my savior and there is no one else like You! Thank You for the gift of salvation. Even if You never did another thing for me, Your saving power is more than enough to make me fall in love with You. I want to see You for who You are and today I say that You are my savior. I was bound for a Godless eternity but You rescued me from that fate.

As my savior, I can rest in the knowledge that You have my life and my future in the palm of Your hands. You have it covered! Thank You that Your salvation continues to rescue me from the wrong decisions I could make every day. What would I have done if it wasn't for Your salvation? You cared about me so much that You came and died for me. What a gift that is and what hope that brings to me today!

Thy kingdom come!

Journal

Go back and remember when you first received salvation. Write down your salvation story and look at how the Lord worked as a savior in your life.

The Trustworthy God

The Lord is trustworthy. 1Cor. 7.25

DAY 2

The Trustworthy God

The Lord is trustworthy. 1 Cor. 7.25

Adoration Statement

Jesus, You are worthy of my trust. There are many people in my life that have failed me but You have never failed me. Even during the times when it felt like You let me down, I now know that I was just seeing things the wrong way. You are trustworthy and I will put my trust in You today. *Lord give me your eyes — give me faith rooted in your goodness and faithfulness,*

Prayer

Lord, I acknowledge that there have been far too many times when I haven't trusted You. Things have happened and I have accused You of not being trustworthy but today I recognize the truth — You are trustworthy! Today, I want to repent by changing the way I think about You. I want to agree with what Your word says about You and not let my circumstances tell me who You are.

Today I take hold of Your promise for my life. You *are* worthy of my trust. You have never let me down, ever! Thank You for leading me every step of the way. Thank You that more times than I admit, You have actually carried me through storms and difficult seasons of my life. Even when it has felt like You were asleep in the boat, You were always with me. I know that just one word from You causes the wind and the waves to cease. I trust You today with my life, my family, my finances and my future.

Journal

Think about the journey of your life. Write down the times you have experienced trial and hardship. Now, take a moment and allow the Lord to show you how He was there for you in the midst of the trial. Write down where He proved Himself trustworthy.

God The Helper

But I tell you the truth, it is to your advantage that I go away; for if I do not go away, the Helper will not come to you; but if I go, I will send Him to you. John 16.7

DAY 3

God the Helper

But I tell you the truth, it is to your advantage that I go away; for if I do not go away, the Helper will not come to you; but if I go, I will send Him to you. John 16.7

Adoration Statement

Holy Spirit, You are my helper. I love when I feel Your Spirit at work in my life, both in times of difficulty and in times of joy. You bring me such hope and fill me with such abundant life! I could not do this life without You being my helper and my friend. What an incredible gift You are! Thank You for always being there with an answer when I need it!

Prayer

Father, thank You for the gift of Your Spirit. When Jesus left the earth, He promised that He would send a helper and that Helper is the Holy Spirit. Holy Spirit, I want to acknowledge Your presence in my life and never leave You out of any circumstance I am faced with. I need Your help every day so that my life will be lived in agreement with the will and the purpose of God.

I have tried to live my life by my own rules and my own opinions far too many times. I know that my desire for independence has not allowed You to be the Helper that You desire to be. Today, I give You the freedom to do what You want! I declare that I will live in agreement with You and listen to You for help today. I want every word and action to be led by You. Let my life be a reflection of someone who is allowing the Helper to do His work in me and through me!

Journal

Write down the areas of your life that have you do not allow the Lord to help you in. Allow the Holy Spirit to meet you in those places and give Him the time and space to be the Helper that He desires to be.

The Good God

Beloved, do not imitate what is evil, but what is good. The one who does good is of God; the one who does evil has not seen God.

3 John 1:11

The Good God

No one is good except God alone. Luke 18.19

Adoration Statement

God, You are good! You are not just good sometimes— You are good all the time! Even when I don't understand what is going on, I will declare that You are good. I have felt Your goodness in my life on so many occasions and I can't help but tell You today, You are good!

Prayer

God, You are good and everything You do is good. When you made the earth, the trees, and the animals, You declared it to be good— and it was! It was good because it came from You! You can't help but be good! There are so many things on this earth that we call good but none of them compare to You. You are the perfect example of what good is.

Even when I don't understand what is going on, You are still good. When I can't make sense of the situation, I will still say that You are good. The circumstances don't change who You are and You are always good. ~~I will not let my opinion of who You are be dictated by what I see with my eyes or hear with my ears~~. I will declare what Jesus said about You in Luke 18.19— ~~You are goo~~d. What a good God we serve!

Journal

Think about how good God has been to you. Take sticky notes and write each good thing God has done for you down on a separate note and spread them around your home or office. Every time you see a note today, stop and tell Jesus how much you love for Him for His goodness.

The Fountain of Living Water

O LORD, the hope of Israel, all who forsake You will be put to shame... because they have forsaken the fountain of living water, even the LORD. Jer. 17.13

The Fountain of Living Water

O LORD, the hope of Israel, all who forsake You will be put to shame... because they have forsaken the fountain of living water, even the LORD. Jer. 17.13

Adoration Statement

Lord, You are the fountain of living water. Every time You speak to me, I am reminded again that true life only comes from You! There have been so many fountains in my life that have promised to satisfy but they haven't. They have only ever left me dry and wanting more. Lord, every drop from You satisfies! You are the fountain that will never leave me dry.

Prayer

Lord, thank You that You are the fountain of life. You are the water that satisfies! I know that the only place I can turn for true satisfaction is You. Water is so important to our natural lives and that is why You described Yourself as the spiritual water that brings life. You are the fountain that I can drink from and be satisfied.

Lord, I confess that there have been fountains that I thought would satisfy me. I thought that having more money or a family or a steady career would satisfy me. The problem is, everything I have tried has only left me more empty than before. I confess that the only place of true satisfaction is You. I come boldly to drink of You and Your presence today. I know that as I do, I will find hope and will never be put to shame.

Journal

Write down the things that you have tried to find satisfaction in (eg. career, family, money, sports, vacation, food, relaxation, entertainment etc). Did they leave you dry? Take a black marker and cover over those areas. Ask the Lord to be satisfied with the fountain of life.

The
Determined
God

For God so loved the world, that He gave His only begotten Son, that whoever believes in Him shall not perish, but have eternal life. John 3.16

DAY 6

The Determined God

For God so loved the world, that He gave His only begotten Son, that whoever believes in Him shall not perish, but have eternal life. John 3.16

Adoration Statement

Father, I am amazed by how determined You are toward me! Your love for me was so great that You gave Your only son to rescue me. You never gave up even when I hated You and wanted nothing to do with You. I stand amazed by Your determination and want to be more like You in my life today!

Prayer

Father, I am so overwhelmed by the way You love me. When I think about what it cost You to rescue me, it brings me to my knees. You never gave up on me! So many people in my life have given up on me, but You never did. You were so determined to have me for Yourself that You gave the most precious gift in heaven for me. You sent Your only Son to die in my place as evidence of how much You loved me and were determined to rescue me.

I know at times I have given up far too easily. Sometimes, the way has been hard and things have seemed too difficult. But, I am motivated today by the way that You never gave up no matter how difficult the road was for You. Even in the garden of Gethsemane, Jesus asked You if there was another way than the cross but He still submitted Himself to Your leadership and was determined to see Your will accomplished. I confess that I want to be like Jesus today. I want to be determined to accomplish Your will in my life just as Jesus did.

Journal

What are the things that have been most difficult for you in the last year? Where do you feel like you gave up? Write down the areas that the Lord is asking you to take a stand and be determined to accomplish His will no matter what the cost.

The Compassionate God

I Myself will make all My goodness pass before you, and will proclaim the name of the LORD before you; and I will be gracious to whom I will be gracious, and will show compassion on whom I will show compassion." Ex. 33.19

The Compassionate God

I Myself will make all My goodness pass before you, and will proclaim the name of the LORD before you; and I will be gracious to whom I will be gracious, and will show compassion on whom I will show compassion." Ex. 33.19

Adoration Statement

God, You are so compassionate toward me! How is it that even though You see everything, You still respond with compassion? I know it is because it is Your nature and Your character to be compassionate. It is a part of Your name. Thank You for Your compassion toward me today!

Prayer

Father, What an overwhelming thing it is to think about Your compassion toward me! When I start to realize how much You really love me and how much You really care about my life, I lift my hands up in thankfulness. Your compassion makes me want to surrender myself even more to You. No one has ever loved me the way that You have or even thought about me like You have.

Even my own parents have not had the kind of compassion You have towards me. You are never disappointed by my failure or my weakness and You understand how frail I really am. The tenderness of the way You love me motivates me to want to love You more in return. You love to show compassion toward me, so I will run into Your compassion today.

Journal

Write down what you consider to be your weakest areas in your life. Ask the Lord if He thinks those things disqualify you from His love (if you hear anything other than a resounding "NO!", then you that is not the Father, it is a lie from hell).

The Building God

Unless the LORD builds the house, they labor in vain who build it. Psa. 127.1

DAY 8

The Building God

Unless the LORD builds the house, they labor in vain who build it. Psa. 127.1

Adoration Statement

God, You are the builder! You love to get Your hands dirty and see things built. You are not afraid of the process and You love to be involved in every part of building our lives, businesses, our families, and our future! I look to You today as the God who builds my life. I make room for You to do what You want to do. I make room for You to oversee the construction of every area of my life!

Prayer

God, You have been the builder of my life in every way— from the blueprints, to the layout, to the construction, right down to the final touches. Your hands and Your spirit have been at work to build me all my life. I could never have done this without You and the areas of my life that are failing are most likely because I didn't allow You, the Builder, to build according to Your plans. Forgive me for the times I have superimposed my plans over Your plans!

I repent of trying to make things happen my own way. I repent of thinking that I had a better plan for my life or my family or my career than Your plan. I have been so wrong! You have always had a better way and I no longer want to build in vain. I want everything that I do to have eternal value and the only way that can happen is by submitting myself to Your leadership as the builder God. Come build my life and my future today!

Journal

Write down the key areas of your life (eg. family, business, career). Now draft a document that hands over the design, building and finishing of those things to Jesus. Sign it and date it!

The Restoring God

He restores my soul; He guides me in the paths of righteousness for His name's sake. Psa. 23.3

The Restorer God

He restores my soul; He guides me in the paths of righteousness for His name's sake. Psa. 23.3

Adoration Statement

God, You are the restorer of my life. Every broken thing, every discarded promise and every forgotten dream is remembered by You. Oh, how You care for my heart and my life today! How great Your tender heart is toward me, even in my weakness! You restore everything in it's time and I trust You today to be the restorer of my soul.

Prayer

God, I confess that there have been many days when I have woken up and not wanted to get out of bed. I have been weary and tired and tried to do so much out of my own strength and ability. But Lord, even when I have grown weary and tired, You have been there as my restorer. When everything in my life seemed too overwhelming, You brought such restoration to my soul.

The way You guide my life is astounding. You know exactly how much I can handle and You never put more on me that I can bear. Even when I feel the overwhelming pressure of life, You bring such a refreshing to my soul. You restore the areas of my life that I have no strength to attend to anymore. I thank You that even when I have forgotten the promises, You haven't. When I have given up, You haven't and You will restore my soul because You are the restorer!

Journal

Write down the things that weigh most heavily on your mind today. Allow the Holy Spirit to bring a restoration of hope to those areas. What is He saying? Does He have a plan for those areas that maybe you haven't thought about? Write down what you hear.

The Perfecter

Fixing our eyes on Jesus, the author and perfecter of faith, who for the joy set before Him endured the cross, despising the shame, and has sat down at the right hand of the throne of God. Heb. 12.2

The Perfecter

---

*Fixing our eyes on Jesus, the author and perfecter of faith,
who for the joy set before Him endured the cross,
despising the shame, and has sat down at the right hand
of the throne of God. Heb. 12.2*

Adoration Statement

Jesus, You make everything perfect because You are the perfecter of
my faith. What an amazing savior I have! Not only have You written the
story of my life, You are also finishing it. How could anyone ever stop
trusting You? Thank You for being the perfecter of my faith today!

Prayer

Jesus, You have been so kind to me. Your unceasing love toward me
makes my heart come alive. I am in awe of Your ways as I look upon
Your character and see the way that You have promised to perfect my
faith. If I trusted in my own ability to make my life and faith work, I

would be in trouble! You are the one who is both writing and finishing the story of my life and my faith.

Jesus, I fix my eyes on You today. I don't want to be distracted by anything else, I want my complete attention to be on You. I fully submit myself to Your leadership and Your plans for my life. My hope and my future is secure because the person who is perfecting my life is faithful and true!

Journal

You are 10 days in! Well done! Take 15 minutes today to do absolutely nothing. Turn the music off, go to a place by yourself and just sit quietly. Don't ask for anything, say anything or pray anything. Just sit and receive His love for You. In your mind, focus on Jesus as the one who both writes your story and finishes the story of your life.

The Truth

Jesus said to him, "I am the way, and the truth, and the life; no one comes to the Father but through Me. John 14.6

The God Who Is Truth

Jesus said to him, "I am the way, and the truth, and the life; no one comes to the Father but through Me. John 14.6

Adoration Statement

Jesus, I love that You called Yourself the truth! When the world considers truth to be a relative concept, You define it according to who You are. I want to search out and know the truth today, the truth that is You. Let my entire life be defined by who You are Jesus.

Prayer

Jesus, You are the Truth. You are not a true concept or an idea that is true—You are truth itself. The whole world around me is trying to define truth according to their own lives and circumstances but You have defined it according to who You are. I thank You that today I have discovered again w=hat the truth is.

Jesus, help me to see You for who You are. I give You the freedom to point out the places that I have believed lies about You and tried to define You by my own circumstances or situations. I give You the freedom to uproot the lies that have taken root in my life because of my failure to see You for who You are. I want the truth to be the defining factor in my life. I want my life to be a reflection of the one who is the Truth. Thank You that You are the truth in my life today!

Journal

Write down the names of God that we have prayed into over the last 11 days on a separate piece of paper. Mark the names that you still struggle to believe are true. Ask the Holy Spirit to reveal Jesus as the Truth in those areas.

The Near God

Draw near to God and He will draw near to you.

James 4.8

The Near God

Draw near to God and He will draw near to you. James 4.8

Adoration Statement

God, You are always near to me. You have never left me or forsaken me no matter what the circumstances have been in my life. I declare that Your nearness to me is my only good. Just like a child, I can lean my head against Your chest and hear Your heartbeat. Thank You that You are near to me today!

Prayer

Jesus, You are near to me in every one of the situations and circumstances I face in my life. When great things have taken place and I have been overwhelmed by Your goodness, You were near to me. When bad things happened and I wondered if I would ever make it through, even then You were still near to me. You are my dearest and closest friend. You know me better than anyone else and You love me better than anyone else ever has.

I feel Your presence even now and want to continue to feel Your presence at all times! Thank You that I am never alone, that I am never forsaken and that I am never far from Your presence. In Your presence is fullness of joy and I long to be near You at all times. My greatest desire is to be close to the one who loves me. I love that You want to be close to me as well! You are not afraid of drawing close to me even in my weakness. Thank You for Your nearness in everything I do today.

Journal

Take a notepad with you wherever you go today. Whenever you feel the presence of God, make note of it. At the end of the day, ask yourself how you can better recognize the God who is near. Think about the times that you were just not aware of Him and make a note to be more conscious of His presence at all times.

God Our Maker

Come, let us worship and bow down, let us kneel before the LORD our Maker.

Psa. 95.6

God Our Maker

Come, let us worship and bow down, let us kneel before the LORD our Maker. Psa. 95.6

Adoration Statement

God, You are my Maker. You are the one who fashions and forms me. You made my personality, my genetic traits, and my family line without ever making a single mistake. You are the author of my future bad you do it with perfection because you understand who I am and where I am going. I trust You and believe in You today as my Maker and my God.

Prayer

Father, You made the heavens and the earth and everything that is in them through Your word. Your creativity is astounding! When I look at Your creation, I am speechless at the wonder of what You have made. Who am I that You even have one thought toward me?

You are a wonderful maker. Everything You make is good and You never make anything that is not good. You never made a mistake when You made me and I am thankful that even the things that I think are flaws are a part of Your perfect plan as my Maker. You perfectly made my life and You are perfectly making my future each day as I walk in faith. God, today I come and worship at Your feet. I am Your creation and You are my Maker.

Journal

Write down a favorite thing you made as a child. How does it make you feel when you think about it? Let the Holy Spirit reveal to you how the Father feels about you as the most favorite thing He has ever made.

The Generous God

Every good thing given and every perfect gift is from above, coming down from the Father of lights, with whom there is no variation or shifting shadow.
James 1.17

DAY 14

The Generous God

Every good thing given and every perfect gift is from above, coming down from the Father of lights, with whom there is no variation or shifting shadow. James 1.17

Adoration Statement

Father, You are so generous toward me! Thank You that every good thing, every perfect gift has come from You and no one else. Thank You that as the generous God, You do not change. You remain generous toward me every day! I lay hold of Your generosity today for my life and my family.

Prayer

Father, how generous You are! Not only did You send Your son to die for me, You also gave me Your Holy Spirit to be with me. Not only did You rescue me from death, You also gave me full and abundant life! You could have stopped at just the bare necessities, but You didn't.

Because of Your great love for me, You continue to lavish love, affection and gifts on me.

Lord I receive of Your goodness and generosity today. I remember all the times in my life when You went above and beyond what I thought was going to happen and I worship You for being the generous God. Thank You that everything You do is good and perfect. Thank You that I can walk today in the knowledge that whatever I need for today will be given to me generously. I will have more than enough to accomplish Your will today because You are the generous God!

Journal

Write down all the things you have that are above and beyond what you really need. Thank the Lord for how generous he has been to you in your life.

The Burden Bearing God

Cast your burden upon the LORD and He will sustain you; He will never allow the righteous to be shaken.

Psa. 55.22

The Burden Bearing God

---

*Cast your burden upon the LORD and He will sustain you;
He will never allow the righteous to be shaken. Psa. 55.22*

Adoration Statement

Lord, You are the one that carries my burdens. You are the one that
sustains me and keeps me all the days of my life. I am so thankful that
the heaviest burdens that have been placed on me can be released
from me right now. I can take the burden off my shoulders and place
them into Your capable hands. Thank You for being my burden bearer
today!

Prayer

Lord, I confess that a lot of my life has been spent trying to carry my
own burdens. Today I repent of trying to bear the load of life on my
own. Today I release all my burdens into the hands of the only person
that can carry them and not be shaken. Today, I cast all my cares

upon Jesus! I take the burden of financial responsibility, the burden of family responsibility and the burden of an uncertain future and I cast it upon the Lord.

Thank You Jesus that as I do this, You have promised that You will sustain me! You said that as I release my burden to You, I will come to a place of such confidence and trust that I will never be shaken. You are my burden bearer! You are my strength when I am weak! You are my hope when all things seem hopeless! Thank You for being my burden bearer today.

Journal

Make a list of the things that keep you up at night and the things that you would consider to be a burden. Tear up the paper and release those things to the burden bearing God! Ask the Lord for divine strategies related to those issues.

The Eternal God

"I am the Alpha and the Omega," says the Lord God, "who is and who was and who is to come, the Almighty."

Rev. 1.8

The Eternal God

"I am the Alpha and the Omega," says the Lord God, "who is and who was and who is to come, the Almighty." Rev. 1.8

Adoration Statement

Lord God, You are the eternal God! You have always existed and You will always exist. Everything that exists in the physical and spiritual world is because of You. You are the beginning and the end. You are the centerpiece of our present world and You will always be. I stand in awe of You today!

Prayer

Lord God, when I take the time to measure my tiny existence in the light of eternity, I get awestruck by how big and awesome You really are. You existed in the beginning when nothing else did. You were before all things and because of You all things exist. I love that I get to discover You as a friend and a savior, but when I think about You as the eternal, majestic God, I tremble at Your greatness.

Open up my eyes today to see beyond the things right in front of me so that I can stare into who You are as the eternal God. I want to rightly measure my life and see You for who You are. Thank you that You desire to reveal eternity to me and You allow me to see beyond the short existence that is my life. You are the beginning and the end! I know how this all ends because I know who You are! What an amazing story!

Journal

Go outside tonight after dark and stare into the stars in the night sky. Think about how far away each of those stars are and how long it takes for the light from those stars to reach earth. Allow your heart to be impacted by the God who made such vast distances and existed long before any of them were made.

The God Who Heals

Bless the LORD, O my soul, and forget none of His benefits; who pardons all your iniquities, who heals all your diseases. Psa. 103.3

The God who Heals

Bless the LORD, O my soul, and forget none of His benefits; who pardons all your iniquities, who heals all your diseases. Psa. 103.3

Adoration Statement

Jesus, You are the healer. Your word tells me in Isaiah 53 that it is by Your stripes that I am healed. You love to heal and just like You healed all kinds of people when You were ministering on the earth, You still love to heal all kinds of people today. I love that You are my God the healer!

Prayer

Jesus, You love to heal because You are the healer. In the Old Testament, the Father revealed Himself to the children of Israel as Jehovah Rapha, the God who Heals. Thank You that You are the fulfillment of that name. Thank You that Your death and resurrection made a way for me to receive healing today for my own life and my family. Thank You that Your blood is enough to heal every disease and every sickness. There is not a single issue that can stand in the way of God the healer!

Jesus, I look to You today as the Healer. You not only heal my body, but You also heal my mind and my emotions. You are in the business of full restoration! I will not grow weary when my healing does not happen when I think it should because the circumstances do not change who You are! You will not in any way fail to fulfill Your Word! Your Word tells me that You heal *all* my diseases and I will believe nothing less today! Thank You that You are my healer!

Journal

Do you have sickness in your body? What about a family member? Pray for that issue today but instead of asking God to heal, just declare who He is over that issue. Tell the issue that it needs to go because of who God is!

The Overcoming God

These things I have spoken to you, so that in Me you may have peace. In the world you have tribulation, but take courage; I have overcome the world.

John 16.33

The Overcoming God

These things I have spoken to you, so that in Me you may have peace. In the world you have tribulation, but take courage; I have overcome the world. John 16.33

Adoration Statement

Jesus, You are the overcoming God. You overcame the devil in the wilderness, You overcame every form of temptation and You even overcame death! There is nothing too great for You! Thank You that there is nothing today that can happen to me that You cannot overcome! You are the overcoming God!

Prayer

Jesus, You are the victorious overcomer! Every trial You ever faced was to show me that we can partake of Your victory and overcome as well. Thank You that You did not run from trials and temptations but You faced them with courage to give me an example to live by. Today I want to live by Your example and face my temptations and trials with courage. Because of Your victory, I can have victory!

Jesus, thank You that because of Your victory, I can have peace. Even if the whole world feels like it is crashing around me, I know that I can rest in confidence knowing that my life is in the hands of the overcoming God. I will no longer be swayed by circumstances, I will be steadfast and will take courage in You. I look to You today for hope and courage because You are the overcoming God!

Journal

Write down the things in your life that would have to change if you were faced with a major crisis. What could you lose? Does this make you fearful? Ask the Holy Spirit to deal with you now so that you are not shaken when trials come.

The Forgiving God

If we confess our sins, He is faithful and righteous to forgive us our sins and to cleanse us from all unrighteousness.
1John 1.9

The Forgiving God

If we confess our sins, He is faithful and righteous to forgive us our sins and to cleanse us from all unrighteousness. 1John 1.9

Adoration Statement

Father, thank You that You are the forgiving God. Thank You that even though my sin can be great at times, I can truly repent and You are so quick to forgive me! You never hold my sin against me because You are faithful to forgive and move on. Your forgiveness is such a gift to me today!

Prayer

Father, You are so gracious. There have been so many times in my life when I have openly sinned against You and yet You still forgive me. If I confess my sin to You, You are quick to forgive me and cleanse me from my sin. Thank You that You don't just overlook my sin, You actually cleanse me from it!

Lord, help me to do my part. Help me to be open and honest with You today about my failures. I don't want to live pretending that everything is ok when it is not. I want You to search my heart and see if there is any wickedness in me. I want to live clean before You because You are so ready to forgive and cleanse me from *all* of my unrighteousness. Today I want to get my life right before You again and allow You to completely have my heart. Thank You for being the forgiving God today!

Journal

Today, be honest with yourself. Ask the Holy Spirit to reveal areas of sin that are keeping you from full obedience to God. Genuinely repent of those things and allow the Holy Spirit to cleanse you. Keep short accounts with God by being honest with Him and not allowing your heart to grow hard by overlooking the sin in your life.

The God Who Has A Voice

The LORD also thundered in the heavens,
and the Most High uttered His voice.

Psa. 18.13

The God Who Has A Voice

The LORD also thundered in the heavens, and the Most High uttered His voice. Psa. 18.13

Adoration Statement

Lord God, You love to speak! When You first spoke, light came forth. It was Your voice that brought forth all of creation and You continue to speak to us even today! Your voice was revealed through the person of Jesus and continues to be heard through the Holy Spirit that lives in us. You are always speaking and I love to hear Your voice as it speaks to me!

Prayer

Lord God, I long to hear Your voice. When I think about creation coming forth because of Your voice, it makes me long to hear from You. When You spoke, the chaos came into order. When You spoke, mountains fell down and the earth gave way. Your voice is mighty and

I want to hear from You today. I want to listen and hear the sound of Your voice as it speaks to me and tells me amazing things about who You are.

Lord God, Your voice changes everything. It was Your voice that spoke to Jesus saying, "this is My beloved Son" and today I want to hear those same words as You speak to me about my life. Your voice is the answer to a world in need. Your voice brings hope and restoration. Your voice sets everything in its right place. Thank You that You are not silent and distant. Thank You that You love to speak to me and tell me about who You are and the plans You have for my life. You are not hiding from me, You are ready and willing to speak to me. So today I will listen for Your voice and I will allow it to thunder through me!

Journal

You are 20 days in! Well done! Take 30 minutes today to do absolutely nothing. Turn the music off, go to a place by yourself and just sit quietly. Don't ask for anything, say anything or pray anything. Just sit and listen to the God who has a voice.

The Understanding God

With Him are wisdom and might; To Him belong counsel and understanding.

Job 12.13

The Understanding God

With Him are wisdom and might; To Him belong counsel and understanding. Job 12.13

Adoration Statement

Father, You understand me! You understand everything about me and my life because You are the understanding God. All knowledge and wisdom come from You, every good idea comes from Your storehouse and to You belongs all counsel and understanding.

Prayer

Father, I bless You today because You understand me. You understand the inner workings of my heart and You understand exactly how You made me and exactly who I am called to be. Your counsel and wisdom are exactly what I need every day. Who else could I turn to for answers when I am in need? My friends don't always understand me, my family doesn't always understand me, but You ALWAYS understand me!

Father, to You alone belongs all the wisdom and might. You see things that I don't see and that gives me great courage to face every day with! I can trust You even when I don't understand because You understand! You understand all that is going on because You see the whole picture. Thank you that as I lean into You today, You will speak to me and give me the ability to see like You do.

Journal

Write down some things that are happening in your life that you don't understand. Ask the Lord to give you counsel about those things. Write down what you feel like He is saying.

The Wise God

To the only wise God, through Jesus Christ, be the glory forever. Amen.

Rom. 16.27

The Wise God

To the only wise God, through Jesus Christ, be the glory forever. Amen. Rom. 16.27

Adoration Statement

God, You are wise! All the greatest men in all the earth could put their wisdom together and it would still only be a drop in the ocean of Your wisdom. Your wisdom gives me solutions to problems that could not be fixed without You. I look to You today, God of wisdom!

Prayer

Lord God, who is there like You? You are the only wise God! So many religions try to point out the wisdom of their gods and leaders but not even one of them comes close to You. Thank you that You make Your wisdom available to me and even today, I can access it whenever I need it. All I have to do is ask You and You will freely give me wisdom from Your immeasurable storehouse of wisdom!

I confess that I have often tried to walk in my own wisdom and not the wisdom of God. I have tried to make things happen my way but You always have a better way because You are so wise! Lord I always want to seek You for wisdom first! I don't want You to be an afterthought, I want You to be the first person I turn to for wisdom and answers. Today I declare You over my life as the God of wisdom and seek You again so that Your wisdom will invade my life.

Journal

Write down the questions that you have that need answering within the next week. Maybe you have a financial need, a family situation or a relational struggle that you don't know how to change or solve. Ask the Lord for His wisdom. How would He approach this situation?

The God With A Plan

The counsel of the LORD stands forever, the plans of His heart from generation to generation.

Psa. 33.11

The God With A Plan

The counsel of the LORD stands forever, the plans of His heart from generation to generation. Psa. 33.11

Adoration Statement

Lord, You are the God with a plan! You always see beyond the immediate situation and You have a plan that spans generations. Your plan extends beyond my life and incorporates my children and grandchildren. Thank You for the plan You have for me today!

Prayer

Lord, when I think about You, I am amazed. I am amazed because You have such a long term plan for my life and my family. Your plan for my life takes into account things that I have not even foreseen coming. Today, I abandon myself to Your plan for my life. I have tried far too many times to make a plan for my life, but I don't have the understanding to be able to see what lies ahead. But You are the God with a plan and You see it all! I will gladly trust my life and my future to You!

Forgive me Lord for not trusting You. Forgive me for leaning on my own ability to plan and get vision for my life instead of asking the God with a plan to speak to me. You know exactly what is coming whether it is good or bad and You know how to help me navigate the road ahead. I put my trust in You today. I want to thank you that You see beyond my life into the future and You know how to best accomplish Your plan. Help me to see the way You see God!

Journal

What are your 3 year, 5 year and 10 year goals? Ask the Lord to speak to you about His plan for you and see if it lines up with your plans. If not, its time to make a change!

The Approachable God

Let us draw near with a sincere heart in full assurance of faith, having our hearts sprinkled clean from an evil conscience and our bodies washed with pure water.
Heb. 10.22

The Approachable God

Let us draw near with a sincere heart in full assurance of faith, having our hearts sprinkled clean from an evil conscience and our bodies washed with pure water. Heb. 10.22

Adoration Statement

Jesus, You are so approachable. Since the day that I said yes to following You, I have always had access to Your heart. I do not have to fear when I approach You because You are calling me to draw near. Thank You that I can have full confidence when I come to because You love me so much!

Prayer

Jesus, You are so approachable. You never turn anyone away no matter what they look like, what they have done, their family history, their political affiliations or the color of their skin! You always welcome us to sit with You and learn from You. Thank You that there is no fear in Your presence. I know that sometimes I blow it and fall into sin but I can just as quickly turn, repent and come to You because You love me and You are for me.

Thank You that even little children are welcome in Your presence. You never turned anyone away and You will never turn me away. Thank you that because of the blood You shed, my heart is clean and I can be confident when I look to You. You don't look at me in any other way than love! You are not angry with me, You are not disappointed with me and You are not ignorant of me. You really care for me! Thank You that You are approachable today!

Journal

What are some things in your life that you think would keep Jesus away from you? Do you have sin or issues that you think are too great or shameful that you can't talk to Jesus openly and honestly about? Ask the Lord to help you approach Jesus about these things with confidence that He loves you and is for you.

The Comforter

I will ask the Father, and He will give you another Helper (Comforter), that He may be with you forever.

John 14.16

The Comforter

I will ask the Father, and He will give you another Helper (Comforter), that He may be with you forever. John 14.16

Adoration Statement

Holy Spirit, You are my comforter. You are the hope that I can lean on when all other hopes have failed. You are my anchor and the voice that speaks comfort to me in the midst of whatever storm may come. Thank You for being a comforter today!

Prayer

Holy Spirit, what a gift You are to me in my life. Whenever trials come and things happen that I don't understand, You always speak a word of comfort that brings hope to my soul. You are the true comforter that knows exactly what to say when I need it. When I face things that seem so inconsistent with what I feel is right, You speak to me and You always bring truth and comfort to my wandering heart.

Thank You for being my comforter. I confess that far too many times I have tried to comfort myself with things in this world. I let food or entertainment or friends or relaxation be my comfort but those things never last. You are the only comfort that will not fail me. You never grow weary of being the comforter! You have more than enough comfort to encourage my soul in any occasion so I put my trust and my hope in You today. Thank You for being my comforter!

Journal

When you need comfort, where do you turn? Is it food, entertainment, relaxation, family, friend? Write down the answers. Ask yourself why you turn to those things first? Make an effort today to invite the Holy Spirit in and allow Him to be your comforter.

The Better Than God

Because Your lovingkindness is better than life, my lips will praise You.

Psa. 63.3

The Better Than God

Because Your lovingkindness is better than life, my lips will praise You. Psa. 63.3

Adoration Statement

Lord God, You are the "better than" God! Everything You do is better than what I would have done. Your plans are better, Your ways are better, Your thoughts are better and Your love is better than mine. I praise You today because You are better than life itself!

Prayer

Lord God, I thank You for everything that You have done for me. When I look back on my life, it is better than I could have ever imagined. If all you had ever done was save my soul, it would have been enough but You had a better plan for me than even just that! You wanted to redeem me, give me a hope and a future and then empower me with Your Holy Spirit to be Your witness on the earth!

I confess that I have tried my own way so many times, but You always had a better way. You have a better plan for my family, my future and my finances. You have opened up the door and given me full access to You and now that I have tasted and seen, I know that Your love is better than life. I would rather have Your love than the best the world has to offer. Everything about You is better than anyone could have ever imagined. I declare this over my life today, You are the "better than" God!

Journal

Ask the Lord to reveal His "better than" plan for your life, your finances, your career and your family. What are the areas that you are allowing a plan that is less than what He is offering you?

The God of Delight

Delight yourself in the LORD; and He will give you the desires of your heart.

Psa. 37.4

The God of Delight

Delight yourself in the LORD; and He will give you the desires of your heart. Psa. 37.4

Adoration Statement

You are the God of delight. Everything about You is a wonder and causes my heart to burst with gratitude for who You are. You delight me with wonders in the morning, pleasure throughout the day and thankfulness in the night. My heart is full because of You Jesus!

Prayer

Jesus, You are the God of delight. You are the reason for everything in me that feels joy and hope and peace and life. When I look at a sunset and feel my heart respond, it is because of You. When I take the time to enjoy friends and family, the real reason my heart is full and overflows is because of You! You are my delight. When I feel anxious or get into despair, I know it is because I have taken my eyes off You and allowed my emotions to be ruled by circumstances and not You.

I want to be more like You Jesus. When I stare into who You are, I feel my heart begin to come alive. You fill me with such delight and I cannot help but respond with love for You. Thank You for the simple things in my life that You have given me. I want everything I do to be a response to my delight in You. I don't want to live with ungratefulness in my heart, I want to live with a heart that is fully alive. I know that as I stare into the God of delight, I can only respond with gratefulness. Thank You that You are the God of delight!

Journal

Write down things that you are grateful for in your life. Allow the Lord to show you his face as the God who delights in you and love to give you these things.

The Excellent God

Having become as much better than the angels, as He has inherited a more excellent name than they. Heb. 1.4

The Excellent God

Having become as much better than the angels, as He has inherited a more excellent name than they. Heb. 1.4

Adoration Statement

Jesus, You are excellent and Your name is excellent. You excel far above all others and there has never been anyone that has ever come close to the majesty of who You are. Lord, who compares to You? I stand in awe of how excellent You are today!

Prayer

Jesus, everything You do is excellent. Your ways, Your thoughts, Your plans - *everything* You do is so much better than I could have imagined was possible. When You created the earth and everything in it, it was very good. Your plan to redeem Your creation was brilliant and so creative, we could never have planned it the way You did. You are excellent in everything You do.

Jesus, I declare today that Your name is excellent. Because of the sacrifice You made and because of Your obedience to the will of the Father, You inherited a name far greater and more excellent than even the angels. I want to stare into Your name and let who You are impact my spirit. I want to be so overwhelmed by Your excellence that I can't help but respond with love for You! Thank You for Your excellent name!

Journal

Write down a list of the people that you admire the most. What is it about them that you admire? Allow the Holy Spirit to speak to you about how those attributes are found in Jesus in a far more excellent way.

The God who Guides

You, in Your great compassion, did not forsake them in the wilderness; the pillar of cloud did not leave them by day, to guide them on their way, nor the pillar of fire by night, to light for them the way in which they were to go.

Neh. 9.19

The God Who Guides

You, in Your great compassion, did not forsake them in the wilderness; the pillar of cloud did not leave them by day, to guide them on their way, nor the pillar of fire by night, to light for them the way in which they were to go. Neh. 9.19

Adoration Statement

Lord God, thank You that You are the God who guides me. Thank You that I do not have to wander around trying to find my own way because I can look to You and You will lead me in Your compassion and You will guide me with Your love. I look to You today as the God who guides me in all of my life!

Prayer

Lord God, You are my guide. You are the hope that I cling to when my life seems so out of control. Thank You that even in the midst of the worst day, I can stop and look to You and You will guide me through and give me exactly what I need to accomplish the day. You never forsake me and You never leave me. You are always with me even when I don't feel You or see You, You are still there!

Lord, You desire to lead me today. Help me to put aside my plans and my ways and give me the courage to trust You even when I don't understand. You were so faithful to lead the children of Israel in the desert and You will be faithful to lead me in whatever comes my way today. Thank You that I can trust Your leadership knowing that whatever You do is for my good. I know that You have my best interest in mind and You will never lead me astray if I trust You and faithfully follow You. Be my guide today!

Journal

Write down the places that you need guidance in your life. Maybe it is a career decision, a relational decision or a financial decision. Allow the Lord to guide you in those things.

The Keeper

The LORD is your keeper; The LORD is your shade on your right hand... The LORD will protect you from all evil; He will keep your soul.

Psa. 121.5,7

The Keeper

The LORD is your keeper; The LORD is your shade on your right hand... The LORD will protect you from all evil; He will keep your soul. Psa. 121.5,7

Adoration Statement

Lord God, You are my keeper! You are the one that protects me on every side and keeps me from evil. You keep my soul from stumbling and even when I do, you make a way of escape for me. Thank You that I can run into You today and find You as my keeper.

Prayer

Lord, thank You that You are my keeper. When I think about my life, I remember so many times when situations could have ended in disaster but You kept me and saved me. You are the only one I can run to and know that when I do, I am safe even if circumstances around me fall apart. Today, I know that the only safe place for me is the center of Your will. When I am in Your will, nothing can harm me or shake me.

I want to run into the safety of Your arms today. I know that the world can be a difficult place. I know that often there is danger on every side. But I am not moved and I am not shaken. I know who You are to me. You are my keeper, You are the one who protects me and wherever I am, there You are with me. Thank You for being my keeper today.

Journal

You are 30 days in! Take 45 minutes today to do absolutely nothing. Turn the music off, go to a place by yourself and just sit quietly. Don't ask for anything, say anything or pray anything. Just sit and allow your soul to be impacted by the God who is your keeper.

The Master

Our only Master and Lord, Jesus Christ.
Jude 1.4

The Master God

Our only Master and Lord, Jesus Christ. Jude 1.4

Adoration Statement

God, You are my master. You are in charge of every detail of my life and nothing ever escapes Your notice. I am Yours today and forever and where You go I will go because You are my master!

Prayer

Lord God, You are my master and I desire to obedient to Your leading and Your direction in all of my life. I know at times that I have made myself my own master but every time that has happened I have ended up in trouble. Today I want to return to You, my master and my God. You are not a controlling or manipulative master, You are a patient and kind master that loves to see my success in life.

At times it seems strange to call You master because everything in me wants to shake off Your leadership and rule my own life. In response to that lie, today I confess that You are in control of my life and You are my master. I want to be obedient to every word that You say. I want to be quick to obey and not allow my own sinful nature to rule my life. I will give you the rightful place that You deserve in my life as my master and allow You to lead me in Your kindness. God, You are my master!

Journal

What are the areas of your life that you find difficult to let go of control over? Maybe it is finances or your children's future. Write down those things. Repent for being your own master and ask the Holy Spirit to teach you how to submit to the leadership of Jesus.

The God of Miracles

God was performing extraordinary miracles by the hands of Paul.

Acts 19.11

The God of Miracles

God was performing extraordinary miracles by the hands of Paul. Acts 19.11

Adoration Statement

You are the miracle working God! From the miracle of creation to the miracle of life, You always do amazing miracles every day even when we are not aware of it. The greatest miracle ever performed was the miracle of our redemption so I praise You today as the God of miracles!

Prayer

God, You are amazing. When I look throughout history, I see how time and time again You have performed miracles for Your people. I read about how You did amazing wonders for the children of Israel to rescue them from Egypt. I read about the times when Jesus walked on the earth and He went about doing miracles, opening blind eyes and deaf ears, making the lame walk and even raising the dead. It is in Your very character to be a miracle working God.

Thank You that what You have done in the past You will do today. You are the same yesterday, today and forever! If You worked miracles for others then I will hold onto who You are today for my own life and believe that You desire to work miracles in my life as well! I look to You today as the God of miracles and believe that You can and will do marvelous things. I will not allow the culture or circumstances to tell me that miracles are not for today. I will believe that You are moving today to perform miracles in my life as the miracle working God.

Journal

Where is it that you need a miracle in your life today? Speak to the circumstance and declare the nature of God as the miracle worker over that issue today.

The Redeemer

As for me, I know that my Redeemer lives, and at the last He will take His stand on the earth. Job 19.25

The Redeemer God

As for me, I know that my Redeemer lives, and at the last He will take His stand on the earth. Job 19.25

Adoration Statement

Lord God, You are my redeemer. I have complete confidence in You today as the God who loves to take broken things and restore them back to wholeness. Everything You do is redemptive! You have not only redeemed my eternal soul, but You also redeem my present and my future. Thank You for being the redeemer today.

Prayer

God, thank You that You are a redeemer. Even at the beginning of creation You took that which was nothing and brought forth something. All throughout history You have redeemed the broken and discarded things and made something beautiful. You are never content just to leave things as they are because You love to bring forth the absolute best. Thank You that You are working in me today to redeem me and bring forth something beautiful in my life and thank You that Your salvation is the ultimate expression of Your nature as a redeemer.

There is no situation too great that You cannot redeem it. There is no relationship to broken that You cannot redeem it. Redeeming things is Your favorite thing to do! Forgive me for the times that I have given up on a circumstance or relationship out of frustration or impatience. You always have a plan to bring forth redemption if we would let You. I trust You in every area of my life today and give You the freedom to be my redeemer!

Journal

What circumstance or relationship in your life needs redeeming? Be open with the Lord and allow Him to show you his nature as the redeemer today. He has a plan and wants to break in as your redeemer!

The Satisfying God

Who satisfies your years with good things, so that your youth is renewed like the eagle.

Psa. 103.5

The Satisfying God

Who satisfies your years with good things, so that your youth is renewed like the eagle. Psa. 103.5

Adoration Statement

Jesus, You satisfy! Everything else in life will leave me wanting more, but You are the water that satisfies. As I search for more of You, I find a place of satisfaction that cannot be found anywhere else. You satisfy my life in every way, thank You for being the satisfying God today!

Prayer

Jesus, You are the water that will cause us to never thirst again. I have drunk from many wells looking for satisfaction but every single one of them has left me wanting more. Even in my spiritual life, I have tried to drink from the wells of spiritual activity at times and even there I have been left wanting more. But every time that I have truly tasted of You, I have been satisfied.

There is no one else like You in all of the earth. You fulfill every need that I ever thought I had and even some needs that I didn't even know existed. I was created by You for You and You alone, so why do I still think that anything else but You could satisfy my soul? Today I turn to the only place of satisfaction I know, I turn to You, the satisfying God.

Journal

Where do you find yourself today? Are you weary and tired? Or are you fully satisfied? Write down where you need to Lord to come and show you Himself as the God who satisfies.

The Triumphant God

When He had disarmed the rulers and authorities, He made a public display of them, having triumphed over them through Him.

Col. 2.15

The Triumphant God

When He had disarmed the rulers and authorities, He made a public display of them, having triumphed over them through Him. Col. 2.15

Adoration Statement

You are the triumphant God! You have never lost a battle or been defeated by any foe. You can only be victorious because it is who You are. Thank You that because You are triumphant, I am triumphant in You today!

Prayer

Jesus, You are truly the triumphant God. There has never been a devil or a man that could unseat You from Your rightful place on the throne of history. Every attempt at overthrowing Your authority and rule has ended in disaster for Your enemies because they failed to recognize that You are always the triumphant God! Your power is unmatched in all of history.

Thank You that You have not only defeated Your enemies but You have disarmed them and then triumphed over them. Your victory was so complete that You threw a celebration and make a public display of Your victory! All glory to You Jesus! Thank You that I can be a partaker of Your triumph and celebration because I am Your child. Your victory is my victory so thank You for being the triumphant God today.

Journal

Where is it that you need a victory in your life today? Speak to the circumstance and declare the nature of God as the triumphant God over that issue today.

The Visionary God

"For I know the plans that I have for you," declares the LORD, "plans for welfare and not for calamity to give you a future and a hope."

Jer. 29.11

The Visionary God

"For I know the plans that I have for you," declares the LORD, "plans for welfare and not for calamity to give you a future and a hope." Jer. 29.11

Adoration Statement

You are the Visionary God. You see far beyond what I see and because of what You see, You know exactly what to do. I trust You completely. I can fully rely on You, I can lean into You and put my hope in You today because You are the visionary God. Thank You for being the visionary God!

Prayer

Lord God, You are the visionary God. You see what I do not see. All throughout history You have had a plan and never once has Your ultimate plan been thwarted. Although the enemy at times thinks he has disrupted Your plans, You always had a better plan that the enemy never saw. You were working behind the scenes to bring forth Your perfect will for my life and the only thing You are looking for is my agreement with You.

Today, I declare my agreement with Your plans. I open up my heart and my life to give You the control that You are looking for from me. I confess at times that I thought my plans were better than Yours, but You had far better plans for my life than what I could come up with. Lord, help me to give in to Your better plan. Help me to take my hands off and allow You to take over my life and my future. You are the visionary God over my life today.

Journal

What do you see coming down the road in 5 years time? Can you adequately prepare for everything? Allow the Lord to show Himself as the visionary God and ask Him to speak to you about what is coming in the next few years.

The Way

Jesus said to him, "I am the way, and the truth, and the life; no one comes to the Father but through Me.

John 14.6

The Way

Jesus said to him, "I am the way, and the truth, and the life; no one comes to the Father but through Me. John 14.6

Adoration Statement

Jesus, You are the way and there is no other way but You. Every other path will lead to death but You are the path to life. Thank You that because You are the way, I can be confident in You and Your leading for my life. I look to You as the way today!

Prayer

Jesus, thank You that You are the way. There have been many wise men and teachers over many generations that have put their hand up and told people that their way was the right way. Many of them said wise things and noble things but there was only one man who proved He was the way by giving up His own life and then resurrecting from the dead. Your death and resurrection are the proof that what You say is true.

Jesus, I look to You as the only way today. I have tried to find my own way at times and that has only ever left me frustrated. Your way is far better than my way and today I commit myself to following Your way. I want to be known, just like the early disciples were, as a "follower of the way". Jesus, You are the way, the truth, and the life. Thank You for Your leadership and direction in my life today and thank You that You lead me in the way!

Journal

Ask yourself whose "way" you have been following for your life? Write down the major decisions that you have made in the last year. Were those a product of your way or God's way? Ask the Lord to become "the way" in your life today.

The Zealous God

The zeal of the Lord of hosts shall perform this.

2 Kings 19.31

The Zealous God

The zeal of the Lord of hosts shall perform this. 2 Kings 19.31

Adoration Statement

You are the zealous God! You are passionate and intentional about everything You do and Your passion is contagious! You are zealous over the plans that You are accomplishing and You are zealous for Your people. Thank You that You are the zealous God today.

Prayer

Jesus, You are the zealous God. Your zeal and passion enabled You to finish the work that You started when You came to the earth to die for my sin and redeem me to Your Father. Your zeal for Your Father's house was so great that it caused You to take up a whip and drive the money changers out of the temple! Who is there like You? Who else has the purity of zeal that can accomplish such great works and yet never once enter into unrighteous anger?

Jesus, let the same zeal that is in You be in me today. Let me be zealous for Your kingdom and Your Father's house just as You were zealous for those things. Allow me to partner with You in Your zeal and feel the way that You felt when You were motivated by love for Your people. You are the zealous God and I am glad that You are zealous for me today!

Journal

Write down the things that motivate you to action (injustice, desire, need etc). Ask yourself if your motivations line up with God's motivations. Ask the Holy Spirit to help you partner with the zeal that Jesus has for His kingdom.

The Faithful God

God is faithful, through whom you were called into fellowship with His Son, Jesus Christ our Lord.

1 Cor. 1.9

The Faithful God

God is faithful, through whom you were called into fellowship with His Son, Jesus Christ our Lord. 1 Cor. 1.9

Adoration Statement

You are the faithful God. You never fail in what You set out to do and You are faithful to complete what You started in me. Your faithfulness is the constant anchor for my soul, it is the confidence I can lean upon no matter what I am faced with. Thank You that You are faithful yesterday, today and forever!

Prayer

Lord God, if I look back upon my life with the right perspective, I can see how incredibly faithful You have been in every season of my life. Never once have You left me alone and never once have You failed me. You have always been faithful because You are the faithful God. You may not do things like I think they should be done, but You always accomplish Your will because You are faithful.

Thank You for being faithful to me. You didn't owe me anything but You have given me so much. Everything that I have is because of Your generous hand and Your faithfulness to supply for my needs. I never want to think that You owe me anything, I always want to live in thankfulness as a response to Your faithfulness towards me. You are faithful in every circumstance and I trust You completely today!

Journal

Write down a list of all the bad things that have happened in your life. Now write next to that list all the times that God has come through. See your history through the lens of His faithfulness today.

The Victorious God

The LORD your God is in your midst, a victorious warrior.

Zeph. 3.17

The Victorious God

The LORD your God is in your midst, a victorious warrior.
Zeph. 3.17

Adoration Statement

You are the Victorious God! You win! Your enemies are defeated and it is just a matter of time until they find out. Thank You that Your victory is my victory and because You are victorious, I am victorious! Thank You for the incredible future that is ahead because You are the Victorious God.

Prayer

Oh Lord my God, as I come to the close of this forty days of hope and prayer, I acknowledge that You are my victory. All of my best plans and hopes pale in comparison to who You are. I have no one else to turn to so I look to You because staring into You and seeing who You are makes me aware of who I am. If You are victorious, then I am victorious! Your victory is my victory.

You are in the midst of everything that I do today. I acknowledge You in my family, my job, my thoughts, my finances, my time and every other area of my life. I never want to separate my spiritual life from everything else I do because I know that You are in the midst of everything I do today. You are the victorious warrior who desires to be a part of everything I do. Thank You for Your victory. Thank You for Your hope. Thank You that I can put my trust in You today and never be ashamed! You are my victory!

Journal

You have done it! 40 days! Your last task is to take one hour today to do absolutely nothing. Turn the music off, go to a place by yourself and just sit quietly. Don't ask for anything, say anything or pray anything. Take your bible and spend an hour with the Lord. This will be the foundation for your future! Write down what you hear him say.

JOURNAL/NOTES

JOURNAL/NOTES

JOURNAL/NOTES

JOURNAL/NOTES

Made in the USA
Columbia, SC
22 July 2018